Uplifting The Ethnic American Spirit

Dr. Ida Greene, Ph.D.

ISBN: 978-1-881165-30-9
Library of Congress Card Catalog Number:

ATTENTION COLLEGES AND UNIVERSITIES, CORPORATIONS, AND PROFESSIONAL ORGANIZATIONS:
Quantity discounts are available on bulk purchases of this book for educational training purposes, fundraising, or gift giving.
For information contact: **P. S. I. Publishers, 2910 Baily Ave. San Diego, CA 92105. (619) 262-9951.**

ACKNOWLEDGEMENTS

I am grateful that I was born an African American female in Pensacola, Florida. I am grateful to be a product of the segregated South; it taught me how to define and affirm my self-worth and self-esteem. Learning to develop a positive self-image was challenging when southern whites in the fifties and sixties treated me as "inferior" and a "nobody." I had to develop a strong sense of self to counter these dominant societal beliefs. I decided to become a "somebody" and chose the path of education to achieve my goal. These experiences helped me develop a passion for maintaining my self-esteem, which was almost destroyed during my time in the segregated South.

I am grateful that my mom, who had a third-grade education, wanted me to achieve more than she did and prodded me daily to get an education. I am grateful for my father who believed in me, always saw possibilities in me, and encouraged me to succeed. He consistently viewed me as a leader and number one. Achieving and accomplishing things gave my father pride and satisfaction. I became the first in my family to graduate from high school, the first to become a registered nurse, the first to achieve a Bachelor's degree, the first to earn a master's degree, and also the first in my family to earn a Ph.D. Today, I am passionate about education, learning, achievement, and improving the self-esteem of children.

INTRODUCTION

To uplift the ethnic American spirit, these are the issues I will address: dating, sexuality, sensuality, racism, integration, interracial dating/marriage, the role of the family, the extended family, what it means to grow up as part of a village, and the sadness I feel over its demise. I include anything I feel will help us remember who we are and why God created us as a race of people. We were created to shake the conscience of humanity. Now we need someone (myself) to awaken us to our true purpose and continue to strive for greatness.

You may see the words Afro-American, African American, or Black interchanged. The word Black is generic. It may be used by persons who are mulatto or of African descent but mixed with another race. Afro-American and African American identify one's connection to the continent of Africa. These titles depict philosophical positions or points of reference used to encapsulate the pent-up feelings of a people struggling to define themselves and to become a free, self-governing people who are in control of their own destiny.

African Americans did not come to this country as free people. They were captured, placed on slave ships, tied and restrained with rope around their wrists, ankles, and bodies, and made to lay side by side as if in a sardine can for the journey from

Africa to the Americas. They landed in Virginia and were sold to merchants in the South who needed hired hands to till their crops and pick cotton. Cotton was the number one commodity in the United States at that time. After they arrived on the shores of America, they were sold as property to the highest bidder.

Reflecting on the inception of African Americans on American soil, it becomes clear that they were treated in a subservient, inhumane manner, which was accepted by society at that time. African Americans were taken in jest and viewed as childlike, comical, and stupid among whites. They lived in fear twenty-four hours a day that if they displeased their slave master, they could be sold against their will to the highest bidder. African Americans had no rights. They were not protected under state or federal laws.

Our society continues to use skin color as a measure of one's acceptance. The ideal worthwhile person is blond, blue-eyed, and may be male or female. The further removed one is from this standard determines his/her not being acceptable. Everything negative or bad is dark or evil; therefore, anyone with a less-than-white complexion will be scorned, rejected, or treated as less than others. There is a belief by some Europeans that Africans and African Americans evolved from the ape/monkey and are, therefore, wild, unruly, uncultured, and animal in nature, with an uncontrolled sex drive. Africans were considered ignorant, stupid, and childlike, with brains smaller in weight and mass than whites. Their undeveloped brains were thought to affect their ability to understand complex information. Also, African Americans were the only ethnic racial group in America who came to this country as indentured slaves and were not free people. In this role, they could not decide for themselves or their family until they were free.

I propose that African Americans/Blacks are unable to resolve the color dilemma by themselves because they were not the creators of the stereotyped, prejudicial beliefs held about them. They did not establish institutionalized racism; likewise, they are not the perpetrators of mass media dissemination about the evils of being Black. Therefore, they are powerless to change a system that victimizes them because of their skin color. Due to years of conditioning, African Americans need the support and aid of all conscious, loving people of the human race to change their deeply ingrained negative self-perception. With improved self-esteem, we begin to act empowered. The more we act empowered, the more we become who we were destined to be: a race of people equal to all people.

The key is an educated, enlightened society that sees them as capable, competent, worthwhile people who are valuable and needed by society. A companion book, Stirring Up the African American

Spirit, touches on issues that affect African American culture such as AIDS, the Black family, parenting, adoption, relationships, homosexuality, gay and lesbian relationships, business ownership, verbal/emotional abuse, domestic violence, and the role of religion in it all.

Ethnic Cultural Introduction:

This book addresses and sheds light on the Ethnic American experience; it is an overview, not thorough documentation. Although slavery is the history of African Americans, other ethnic groups have also faced dehumanization and marginalization by the dominant Anglo-Saxon Caucasian society. Yet, some ethnic cultures have chosen to identify themselves as White, Anglo-Saxon. This book will address a few other ethnicities' general cultural attitudes and beliefs.

TABLE OF CONTENTS

CHAPTER 8

CHAPTER 1

The African American Past Revisited

American culture has many generalized erroneous perceptions of African Americans. These perceptions are negative, limited, restrictive, fear-laden, and stereotypical. Modern-day African Americans are products of African culture from the continent and a complex mixture of the Confederate South. Most slaves were separated from their families and sold individually rather than as a family. They were established in the homes of slave masters. Many had kind slave masters, but most experienced abuse. Not all slaves were respected and thought to be stupid and without intelligence. They came from different tribes and spoke the language of their tribe. They did not know how to speak or read English. Most of them were forbidden to learn to read. Many caring children sneaked and taught slave children how to read. Some Africans, like Phyllis Wheatley, learned to read on their own. This gave them a feeling of competence and self-respect and added to their positive self-image and self-esteem.

The African settlers to America were uprooted from their families on both shores of Africa and after they arrived in the United States. They were considered unintelligent, childlike, easy to scare, wild, and like untamed animals. They were placed in chains like animals and sold on an auction block. This was degrading and dehumanizing. It accomplished the intended objective, which was to instill fear, inferiority, and a mindset of servitude and enslavement. Additionally, whites were considered the elite, and slaves were thought of as monetary property. They were valued for their brute strength and ability to work long hours in the sun. Slaves did not have the right to disagree with a request or demand made upon them; neither could they refuse the demand of anyone who was white. Even if the person was a child, Angela Y. Davis, in Women, Race, and Class, wrote, "Females, slave women were inherently vulnerable to all forms of sexual coercion. The most violent punishments of men consisted of flogging (beatings) and mutilations. Most women were flogged, mutilated, and raped. Rape was a camouflaged expression of the slaveholder's economic mastery and the overseer's control of Black women as workers.

In 1860, there were 488,070 free African Americans and 4 million enslaved Africans in America. Most of them could not read or write and had to learn any way they could. They used the Bible or relied on abolitionist people who were against slavery and young white children. Many stole books from the private libraries of their masters or whites who employed them. They sought out other African Americans who could read and write. According to

Carter G. Woodson's "The Negro in Our History," in the 1700s Harry and Andrew, whose last names are unknown, started a school for slaves in Goose Creek Parish, South Carolina, becoming the first African-Americans employed as teachers. During the early years of America's history, skin color was not as important as it has become. As the country grew, wealthy white landowners decided to institute a more profitable employment system called slavery. Africans were forced into slavery. The white men who established this system declared Africans as inferior and sub-human, making skin color the most important human characteristic in America. Skin color determined who received respect and who was treated as a person. One's self-worth was based on skin color. Slaves were forbidden to learn to read or write. Therefore, the self-esteem and self-image of African Americans are rooted in shame about one's skin color and self-doubt about one's intelligence or ability to think.

African Americans have always been valued for what they did, not for who they were. Thus, one's ability to contribute to humanity has always been associated with their performance. African American women, men, and children were treated like children regardless of their age, and all whites were considered their masters. African Americans of all ages referred to white children as "mister" and "miss." This practice contributed to the destruction of their sense of self-worth, self-appreciation, and self-respect. It is self-degrading for an adult Black man to say "yes sir" and "no ma'am" to a child the same age as his own, whom he expects to respect. Acting in this manner puts the man on the same level as his child and reinforces the notion that he is less than a man. A man-child is not a real man because he has no control over his life, his family's welfare, or the circumstances they face. I witnessed my father placed in this situation during my childhood, which made him very strict and demanded respect from all five of us and my mom.

In the past, the Black man thirsted for self-respect but had a shattered, distorted self-concept and self-image. Any attempts to develop self-respect or self-pride were further eroded through institutionalized racial segregation. This separation between Blacks and Whites was evident in all public establishments, including public water fountains. In Pensacola, Florida, where I grew up, Blacks were not allowed to eat at lunch counters with whites, drink from the same water fountains, try on shoes in shoe stores, attend the same schools, live in the same neighborhoods, or sit in the front seats of public transportation. Signs designated areas as "white" and "colored." This was a normal practice in Pensacola, Florida, until 1969. A young Black British journalist wrote, "I'm foreign, so I do not have the legitimate traumatic baggage that African Americans have with (racism), even though I can see it all going on. I've got different traumas… I did get a whiff- which I knew intellectually, but it rarely came to the forefront like this- the fact that white people in the South don't give a damn if I'm British or not. In 1970, I stopped to ask for directions from three elderly white people, and they threatened to shoot me; one of them even went to get his gun. That's when I left. I thought, 'They're not going to shoot me.' Why would they do that? But then I thought, 'Well, maybe they will'; this was an eye-opening experience for me." Because of all the emotional abuse I endured in the South, I still find myself struggling at times with low self-esteem, feelings of low self-worth, and a distorted self-image that tells me I am inferior to whites.

One cannot be chained in shackles all their lives, abruptly have the physical and emotional shackles removed, and then be told they are free human beings. Adults are no longer "children" and begin thinking and behaving as independent free adults. It is easy to remove a physical shackle or chain. However, it may take centuries to unchain a shackled mind. The mind and psyche of all African Americans, whether they lived in the liberal North or the Ku Klux Klan or Confederate South, continue to be shackled and chained due to years of conditioning.

All African Americans living in the South lived in fear of overstepping their boundaries, of getting out of 'their' place and being reminded through a stare, a cold shoulder treatment, or emotional isolation that they were still sub-human and undeserving of respect as human beings. It is very challenging to remove the mental or emotional shackles of an enslaved mind that send out continual messages: "Beat up on me," "I am not okay, but you are okay," "I am worthless," "I need someone other than myself to validate me," "I am not sure if I am as smart as whites or other races of people," "I can't think to figure things out for myself, I need to use the brains of someone other than myself," "My brains are no good and will therefore not work for me," "I am not as valuable as whites," "I am stupid," "I am inferior," "My mind won't work for me, you do not like my looks, and neither do I," "My skin color is dark, my lips are thick, my nose is wide and large, I do not look like those I see on television or the magazine covers, and I am different," "I wish my skin color were lighter, I wish I were a lighter skin color," "There is something abnormal about my skin coloration." When we were children, innocently playing, we told each other daily, "If you are brown, stick around; if you are black, step back; if you are white, you are alright." All of these are self-denial and self-rejection phrases. I remember buying a container of skin-bleaching cream as a teenager to lighten my skin. Even though I was a pretty shade of brown, I did not see or acknowledge this until it was pointed out by a white friend who later lived in San Diego, California, in the 1980s.

In Pensacola, Florida, I could not be seen playing with my white friend as a child. It was acceptable for us to be friends with her mother; however, her mother asked that we not be seen together in public because she feared what might happen to her daughter. I was considered inferior to a fourteen-year-old white girl. Can you imagine the emotional scarring an innocent action like this produces? I have been working on my self-esteem since I left Pensacola, Florida, healing one layer at a time. Due to the conditioning factor of spaced repetition, our mind remembers and retains what it hears. Our minds retain all information, whether to our benefit or not. You must only reject yourself once to set a self-denial, self-rejection pattern in motion. Blacks are ridiculed and humiliated by whites and other races of people. In turn, we ridicule, humiliate, and reject ourselves and other Blacks. This is a behavior we need to be mindful of and avoid.

Other Ethnic Cultural Lifestyles

ASIANS

Asia's history features significant developments seen in other parts of the world and events that have affected those regions. These include the Silk Road trade, which spread cultures, languages, religions, and diseases across Afro-

Eurasia. Another significant advancement was the innovation of gunpowder in medieval China, later developed by the Gunpowder Empires, primarily the Mughals and Safavids, leading to advanced warfare with firearms.

The culture of Asia encompasses the diverse customs and traditions of art, architecture, music, literature, lifestyle, philosophy, politics, and religion practiced and maintained by the continent's numerous ethnic groups since prehistory. Identifying a specific Asian culture or universal elements among its immense diversity originating from multiple cultural spheres and three of the four ancient river valley civilizations is complex. Asia divides into six geographic sub-regions with observable commonalities: culture, religion, language, and relative ethnic (racial) homogeneity. These regions are Central Asia, East Asia, North Asia, South Asia, Southeast Asia, and West Asia.

Filipinos Culture

Filipinos' primary ancestors are Malays who came from the south-eastern Asian country, which is now called Indonesia. The Philippines is a combined society, both singular and plural in form. It is singular as one nation but plural in that it is fragmented geographically and culturally. The country consists of Christians, Muslims, other religious-ethnolinguistic groups, and urban and rural people; between upland and lowland people; and between the rich and the poor. Although different in numerous ways, the Filipinos are very hospitable and respect everybody regardless of Race, Culture, and belief.

Japanese Culture

Japanese society is highly collectivistic, with individuals often viewing themselves as members of groups rather than autonomous individuals. These groups define their members and demand loyalty, providing a sense of belonging, protection, and unity in return. Japan is one of the world's most homogeneous societies, with over 98% of its population sharing the same Japanese ethnicity. There is a strong national identity rooted in a common heritage, history, and cultural identity. Japanese people generally expect their views and behaviors to align with those of other Japanese around them.

Chinese Culture, Tradition and Customs

Present-day Chinese culture is an amalgamation of ancient traditions and a westernized lifestyle. These two coexist like the traditional Yin Yang formula of balance. This contrast is evident in the fashion of the conventional Chinese Qipao dress juxtaposed with towering skyscrapers alongside heritage buildings, and the popularity of both Western dim sum and McDonald's.

Ancient Chinese culture dates back more than 5,000 years and boasts immense diversity and variety in its history. The sophisticated Chinese civilization has made significant contributions to the arts, sciences, including elaborate painting, printing techniques, delicate pottery, sculpture, and revered architectural traditions worldwide. Chinese language, literature, philosophy, and politics continue to exert a strong influence. Chinese culture managed to maintain its unique identity until the advent of Western culture in the mid-19th century.

Chinese Religion, Philosophy, and Politics:

Confucianism, Taoism, and Buddhism have left a lasting impression on Chinese culture and tradition. Confucianism emphasized "Ren" (love) and "Li" (rituals), promoting respect for society and social hierarchy. Taoism advocated a philosophy of inaction, while Buddhism stressed the importance of achieving self-emancipation through good deeds.

RELIGIOUS EXPERIENCES

Filipinos Religion

Due to early colonization by the Spanish, the Philippines is predominantly a Roman Catholic nation, with 81 percent of the population identifying as Catholic, according to the Pew Research Center. Other religions represented include Protestants (10.7 percent), Muslims (5.5 percent), and other Christian denominations (4.5 percent). Approximately 1 percent of Filipinos are Hindu, and another 1 percent are Buddhist.

The Muslim population predominantly resides in the southern provinces of Mindanao, Palawan, and the Sulu Archipelago, often referred to as the Moro region, practicing predominantly the Shafi'i sect of Sunni Islam. Some of the Negrito peoples adhere to traditional animist religions.
https://www.thoughtco.com/the-philippines-facts-and-history-195655

The Philippines is one of the two predominantly Roman Catholic nations in the Asia-Pacific region. The Filipino tradition of attending church and frequent prayer reflects their deep faith and religious beliefs. Many Filipinos demonstrate profound devotion, sometimes risking their lives to participate in events such as touching the Black Nazarene in Quiapo, Manila. For many, these acts symbolize a profound connection between their faith and their fears.

Filipinos believe that having an intense devotion may lead to a better life and guidance to face everyday life.

Japanese Religion

Shinto and Buddhism are Japan's two major religions. Shinto is as old as Japanese culture, while Buddhism was imported from the mainland in the 6th century. Since then, the two religions have coexisted relatively harmoniously and have even complemented each other to a certain degree. Today, most Japanese people consider themselves followers of Buddhism, Shintoism, or both.

Religion does not play a significant role in the everyday life of most Japanese people today. The average person typically observes religious rituals at ceremonies such as birth, weddings, and funerals, may visit a shrine or temple during New Year, and participates in local festivals (matsuri), many of which have religious origins. https://www.japan-guide.com/e/e629.html

Chinese Religion

Confucianism, Taoism, and Buddhism are the three major religions in China, although it is accurate to classify Confucianism more as a philosophical school than a religion.

American Indian Religion

Native American religions are rich and varied, with each tribe maintaining its own distinct set of beliefs and practices. These spiritual traditions are deeply intertwined with nature, reflecting a profound respect and reverence for the natural world. Central to many of these religions is the belief in a creator or multiple creators, who are often seen as the source of all life and existence.

For example, the Iroquois have a spiritual belief system that centers around a creator known as the Great Spirit, a powerful entity that embodies goodness and oversees the universe. Similarly, the Ojibwe people hold a deep reverence for a creator they call the Great Mystery, an enigmatic and sacred force that is the origin of all creation. These creators are not distant deities but are intimately involved in the lives of the people and the natural world, guiding and sustaining all life. Each tribe's religious practices and ceremonies are designed to honor these creators and maintain harmony with the natural world, ensuring the balance and well-being of their communities.

Hispanic/Mexican

Hispanic and Mexican religions are incredibly diverse, reflecting a rich tapestry of influences from Catholicism, indigenous traditions, and African spiritual practices. This blend of religious beliefs has created a unique and multifaceted spiritual landscape. One prominent example of this syncretism is the Day of the Dead, a deeply significant holiday celebrated in

Mexico. During this festival, families come together to honor and remember their deceased loved ones through various rituals and offerings. Altars, known as ofrendas, are elaborately decorated with photographs, favorite foods, and personal items of the departed. These celebrations are not somber, but rather vibrant and joyous, featuring parades, music, and dance. The Day of the Dead exemplifies the harmonious integration of different cultural and religious influences, illustrating how Hispanic and Mexican spiritual practices are a living, evolving tradition that honors the past while embracing the present.

CHAPTER 2

Relationships

Cultural Relationships

Filipinos are among the most hospitable people you may find anywhere. Foreign visitors to the country are treated with the utmost respect. This trait is particularly evident during fiestas and holidays, when Filipinos do their best to entertain their guests.

Amazingly, even the simplest homes along the road open their doors to strangers. For Filipinos, being able to serve others honors true friendship. Filipino hospitality is a trait you can't take away from them.

Japanese: Dating and Marriage

Dating practices in Japan are similar to those in Western cultures. Children usually start dating around 15 but typically marry at an average age of 26-27. When a couple does marry, the wedding can be very elaborate. The bride and groom may have multiple outfits for photographs and the ceremony, ranging from traditional kimonos to modern dresses. Guests may give typical wedding gifts or money to the couple and may even receive a gift from the couple.

Chinese: Dating and Marriage

Couples often meet through mutual friends or social gatherings. However, online dating and matchmaking are becoming increasingly popular. Intimate relations and public displays of affection are discouraged throughout the country but are becoming more common in cities. According to a general health report, the percentage of the population engaging in premarital intercourse increased from 40% in 1994 to 71.4% in 2012. More than half of the younger Chinese population no longer consider virginity at marriage a serious matter. However, there is a generational divide on this issue. Intimate relations solely for pleasure are still discouraged or forbidden by many educational institutions and parents. Virginity remains a prerequisite for some Chinese marriages, and a bride's husband and family may request proof of it.

Filipinos : Dating and Marriage

In the Philippines, dating often comes in stages, beginning with courtship. Typically, a man will try to impress a woman by courting her. If the woman considers the man to be a good suitor, they will continue dating. Individuals have significant freedom in choosing marriage partners, although the family's preferences may influence the choice of a spouse. In some families, the prospective partner is expected to gain the approval of their potential in-laws. However, in urban areas, dating and marriage practices tend to be less conservative and are becoming more influenced by the West.

American Indian: Dating and Marriage

My interest in American Indian culture stems from my grandfather. My granddad described himself as a member of the Cherokee Indian tribe. He had light brown skin, high cheekbones, and dark wavy hair. We never talked about or knew anything about American Indian culture because he died at a young age. My grandmother was a tall, black-skinned woman with tightly curled hair who said she was a proud member of the African Watusi tribe. My grandmother lived to the age of 77, so I heard a lot about her proud roots as an African Watusi, and she dared anyone to mess with Bell Ulmer.

Indian Americans often blend traditional Indian cultural practices with contemporary American norms in their approach to dating and marriage. Traditionally, marriage in Indian culture has been seen as a union not just between two individuals but between two families. Arranged marriages, where families play a significant role in selecting a suitable partner, have been common practice. These arrangements are often based on factors such as caste, religion, social status, and horoscopes. However, the practice of arranged marriages is evolving, with many families now allowing their children to have a significant say in choosing their partner, sometimes opting for a "semi-arranged" marriage where the family approves of a partner chosen by the individual.

In contrast, younger Indian Americans, particularly those born and raised in the United States, are increasingly adopting dating practices similar to those of their American peers. They often meet potential partners through social events, online dating platforms, and mutual friends. While premarital relationships and dating are more common among the younger generation, there is still a strong emphasis on family approval and involvement in the marriage process. Marriage ceremonies often incorporate traditional Indian rituals, such as the "saptapadi" (seven steps) and "mangal pheras" (circling around the sacred fire), reflecting the enduring influence of cultural heritage even as practices adapt to the modern context.

Hispanic/Latino Americans: Dating and Marriage

Family is a central component of Hispanic culture, with "familismo" emphasizing close-knit relationships and loyalty to the family. This cultural aspect significantly influences dating and marriage practices, with family approval and involvement being common. Traditional norms often include formal courtship, where men show respect and seek the approval of the woman's family. Marriage is considered a significant milestone, frequently celebrated with elaborate Catholic ceremonies and extensive festivities. Traditional rituals, such as the "pedida de mano" and the exchange of "arras" (thirteen gold coins), symbolize commitment and the union of two families.

However, dating and marriage practices are evolving among younger Hispanic Americans, who blend traditional customs with contemporary practices influenced by mainstream American culture. While older generations may adhere closely to traditional norms, younger individuals adopt more individualistic approaches, reflecting broader societal changes. Despite these shifts, many still hold onto core values of respect, family unity, and cultural heritage, maintaining a balance between honoring tradition and embracing modernity.

CHAPTER 3

History of the Family

Some African Americans bought their freedom from their slave masters. An industrious and persevering individual was Alonzo Herndon, who lived from 1858 to 1927 and turned $11.00 in savings into a fortune, becoming America's first African-American millionaire. He started as a barber with only white clients. He wrote, "I started alone with a five-chair shop. By unceasing watchfulness of my business and tactfulness, I showed manly conduct toward my Southern patrons, with whom I am happy to say I have always had the most pleasant esteem and have every reason to believe my business is held. I have grown from five barber chairs to twenty-five, employing nearly forty men."

When the state passed a law in 1905 requiring insurance companies to deposit $5,000 with the treasurer, Mr. Herndon purchased nine small burial associations. He organized them into the Atlanta Mutual Insurance Association. That association later became the Atlanta Life Insurance Company, now the nation's second-largest African-American life insurance company. Atlanta Life provided insurance and mortgages to low-income Blacks who could not obtain these services elsewhere. The company also offered African Americans professional, managerial, and clerical jobs. Mr. Herndon was worth $1.1 million at his death in 1927.

Children, as well as adults, learn from society about their self-worth, self-image, and self-importance. If references have been made and put in print that they have the brain of an ape, that they are the offspring of a gorilla, or that their brain mass is smaller than that of whites, if everything said about them in books is negative or degrading, they will eventually believe it. Also, if a person is told or made to believe a given statement is factual, even though it may be a conjecture with limited evidential fact, it will be accepted as true by the mind. This is especially true if the information is stated over a medium such as television

.

Self-esteem is a blueprint of who we are and how we have been treated, respected, appreciated, and identified by those around us and our external family. The self-image is a by-product of self-esteem. It reflects how we picture ourselves and how we honor, respect, and value ourselves. It paints a mental picture of our inner beliefs of who we think we can be or what we can do in life. These words by a noted speaker address self-worth. A well-known speaker started his seminar by holding up a $20.00 bill. In a room with 200 people, he asked, "Who would like this $20 bill?" Hands started going up. He said, "I will give this $20 to one of you, but first, let me do this." He proceeded to crumple up the 20-dollar bill. He then asked, "Who still wants it?" Still, the hands were up in the air. "Well," he replied, "What if I do this?" And he dropped it on the ground and started to grind it into the floor with his shoe. He picked it up, now crumpled and dirty. "Now, who still wants it?" Still, the hands went into the air. "My friends, we have all learned a very valuable lesson. No matter what I did to the money, you still wanted it because it did not decrease in value. It was still worth $20."

Many times in our lives, we are dropped, crumpled, and ground into the dirt by the decisions we make and the circumstances that come our way. We feel as though we are worthless. But no matter what has happened or what will happen, you will never lose your value. Dirty or clean, crumpled or finely creased, you are still priceless to those who love you. The worth of our lives comes not in what we do or who we know but by who we are. You are special; always remember this.

Jesus and the Black Church

You may not relate to the Black American religious experience, but you can relate to your religious foundation being compromised for various reasons. Many of their religious practices have been exaggerated or misinterpreted.

Many African Americans fail to integrate faith and life. We hear a lot about how Jesus died and rose again, but we don't often hear how this affects us daily. Think about how your religious practices intersect with your lifestyle and your personal and work life. The African American culture relies heavily on Biblical scriptures. However, they are not often applied in dating, marital relationships, or communication with each other and how to handle financial affairs to generate wealth. There needs to be a greater understanding of how faith and life intersect in all cultural societies, especially in the African American culture.

Systemic Injustice

The primary culprit behind the Church's lack of influence in the community is old systemic injustice. Black communities in the inner city are the way they are because of decisions that were made years ago. Whether it was poor and inadequate housing or the choice to build freeways over thriving neighborhoods, most problems boil down to systemic injustice, which still exists.

Lack of Connection With Youth

In the eyes of leadership and older members of some churches, traditions are not to be tampered with. Some of the traditions in African American churches are irrelevant to many young people and sometimes create a cultural disconnect that can get in the way of effective ministry.

A Bigger Vision

Also, a lack of vision beyond the Sunday morning sermon prevents some Black churches from having a larger societal impact.

The bigger mission for African Americans is to develop younger leaders who can move them forward with the next generation of new leadership to create a leadership pipeline. Many older preachers and other leaders have held on to their positions and are not training the next generation to replace them. So they will have someone to succeed them when they're gone and who can multiply their efforts in the present by recruiting and training younger leaders.

Filipinos: Family

Having close family ties is also one of their unique traits. It is one of the outstanding cultural values that Filipinos have. The family takes care of each other and is taught to be loyal to family and elders by simply obeying their authorities. This is one of the unique characteristics of Filipinos. Having a fondness for family reunions during secular and religious holidays such as Christmas, New Year's Eve, All Saints' Day, Holy Week, fiestas, homecomings, birthdays, weddings, graduations, baptisms, funerals, etc., is evidence that Filipino people value not only our cultural tradition but the spirit of our family. As Filipinos, we are blessed to have been brought up with strong family ties.

Filipinos highly value the presence of family more than anything. Adult children living with their parents is another Filipino tradition that makes them exceptional. Unlike in the United States, where children leave their homes after finishing high school or college, many Filipinos continue living with their parents until they get married. Religious faith is not often addressed in this culture. Japanese: Family

The Japanese feel a heightened sense of belonging and loyalty to their family as interdependence is emphasized in the collectivist society. Individuals are expected to serve their family's interest before their own and show preferential treatment to fellow family members. Furthermore, families also have a collective face in Japan. The act of a single individual impacts the perception of one's family name by others.

The typical Japanese household follows the nuclear family model; however, the extended family is usually kept nearby and is visited often. Paternal grandparents may live with their family as they age, but Japan's small living spaces limit multigenerational household situations. Religious faith is not often addressed in this culture.

Chinese: Family

The family unit is considered one of the most central institutions. For many, their family gives them a sense of identity and a strong support network. In China, the family is primarily understood through Confucian thought. In Confucian thinking, the family contains the most important relationships for individuals and forms the foundation of all social organization. For instance, the roles of husband and wife, parent and child, and elder brother and younger brother are clearly defined. A husband/father is expected to exhibit dominance and kindness to his wife for obedience and love and offer guidance and protection to his children in return for respect and obedience. Religious faith is not often addressed in this culture.

American Indian: Family

Contact with Europeans brought significant changes to American Indian family life, often leading to misunderstandings and misinterpretations of indigenous customs. European misconceptions included viewing dowry practices as purchasing brides, contrasting with American Indian traditions of demonstrating ability to support a wife through gifts. Many American Indian cultures were matrilineal, with women sometimes inheriting leadership roles, a concept Europeans found unfamiliar and disapproved of. Child-rearing practices differed as well; American Indian children received affection and education rather than European-style punishment. The division of labor also varied greatly: women managed agriculture and household tasks, while men engaged in hunting and warfare. European settlers' emphasis on male roles due to the economic value of hides and furs overlooked the equal contributions of both genders in indigenous societies.

Furthermore, European colonization introduced diseases and displacement, leading to high mortality and population decline among American Indians. This demographic upheaval, coupled with land loss, pushed many tribes to near extinction, as evidenced by Thomas Jefferson's observations of dwindling populations and cultural erosion among the Mattaponies and Pamunkies.

Hispanic/Mexican

Hispanic family values are deeply rooted in closeness, support, and tradition, contrasting starkly with American norms. Latino families emphasize extended family ties, often residing in close proximity and frequently hosting relatives despite space constraints. Moral obligations drive support for family members in need, from financial aid to caregiving. Values like etiquette, respect (reflected in formal language use), and communal dining rituals (sobremesa) are cherished. Religion plays a central role, with Catholicism shaping holidays and daily life. Gender roles vary but typically involve the father as provider and authority figure, while mothers are revered for their nurturing roles. Hispanic values contrast with American ideals of early independence, dispersed families, convenience in meals, and strict punctuality.

CHAPTER 4

Cultural Relationship to Money

Filipino: How do they handle finances, and what does money mean in their societies?

Money is a very sensitive topic for Filipinos. It is unlikely that a Filipino will be very willing to seek help from a financial advisor or attend a financial seminar for advice on improving their financial situation. Instead, they may seek financial advice from family members and significant others rather than from financial professionals who have expertise in the topic.

Many Filipinos do not allocate their money based on priority. Although many say that their family's health is a priority, their actions often state the opposite. Most do not get health insurance or medical cards besides PhilHealth and their employer's provider since this requires a lot of paperwork. The importance of health insurance is often only realized once a critical illness or sudden health problem hits the family.

Resources are often directed towards siblings' or children's education and cultural festivities such as birthday celebrations for every social circle and Christmas gifting. There is also the temptation of buying items for instant gratification, such as gadgets,

instead of saving money for rainy days.
Chinese

The average Chinese household dynamic has evolved away from the traditional archetype as the country has modernized and advanced technologically. Financial success is now a key status symbol. The implementation of the Chinese government's one-child policy meant that for years, the family's prospects rested largely on the shoulders of their only child. While the policy was phased out in 2015, and parents can now have more than one child, most are still utterly devoted to their children's success. They ultimately want to see their children become more prosperous than themselves. Therefore, receiving a good education and attending university is highly regarded, often placing heavy expectations on the child to excel in meeting their parents' aspirations.

Today, some Chinese believe that love is shown through providing money to family members. Less focus is placed on personal bonding as parents work harder and longer to earn more money. More mothers are becoming full-time workers, and fathers are often absent due to work-related commitments. It is common for young children to be raised by their grandparents while their parents work away from home. As such, quality family time is scarce. Chinese families often aim to build or buy a house, as homeownership represents a higher status. These goals entail saving for many years, being thrifty, and carefully managing money as top priorities for the average Chinese family.

Japanese

Japanese households are well known for preferring cash, which represents most of their financial assets. On the surface, this seems like a rational choice in an economy experiencing persistent deflation. Moreover, an aversion to risk appears rational in the wake of Japan's traumatic equity and real estate market collapse in the late 1980s, from which the country still has not recovered. However, Japanese households were stockpiling cash well before the 1990s.

Most children in Japan receive their first training in personal finance at a young age from their parents. They are taught that the more money they save, the higher the quality of personal items they can buy in the future. It is common for Japanese parents to urge their children to keep their 'otoshidama' (traditional cash gifts received from relatives and friends) in the bank to avoid impulse buying. Most parents instill in their children that borrowing money from people is frowned upon in Japanese society. Consequently, high school students often get part-time jobs to fund purchases outside the family budget. Over time, their money management skills improve, so when a man starts his career and raises a family, he is well prepared to manage his finances.

American Indian

In American Indian cultures, the concept of wealth extends beyond monetary value to encompass relationships, nature, and community well-being. This holistic perspective profoundly influences resource management practices. American Indians often view money not just as a means of personal gain but as a tool for ensuring the welfare of the entire community. The communal obligation to share resources is deeply ingrained, guiding the allocation of money and placing significant demands on available resources. This principle of communal sharing reflects a strong sense of responsibility to family and tribe, prioritizing the collective over individual wealth.

Moreover, spirituality and a deep connection to nature are integral to American Indian financial values. These cultural beliefs emphasize sustainable practices that respect the environment and uphold spiritual traditions. For instance, the use of natural resources is often guided by principles of stewardship and respect for the Earth, ensuring that actions today do not harm future generations. Financial decisions are thus made with a long-term perspective, balancing immediate needs with the preservation of cultural and environmental integrity. This approach to money and resources highlights the distinctive values of American Indian communities, which prioritize harmony, sustainability, and communal well-being over individual financial success.

Hispanic/Mexican

Hispanics exhibit distinct cultural attitudes towards money and financial planning that diverge from mainstream American perspectives. While Americans may view having "enough to get by" negatively, Hispanics often prioritize providing basic necessities for their families as a cherished achievement. This immediacy in financial outlook stems from a belief in fatalism and a reliance on faith for the future, influencing their preference for immediate consumption over long-term investment. This behavior is evident in their strong consumption of electronics and household appliances, which enhance their quality of life and family cohesion in the present. Despite their substantial purchasing power in certain consumer goods, Hispanics generally show reluctance towards long-term financial instruments like retirement plans or stock investments, preferring instead to allocate resources towards familial support, both locally and abroad. For financial industries aiming to engage this market, overcoming historical distrust of banking institutions through targeted educational campaigns that build trust and demystify financial services is essential for fostering lasting relationships and changing perceptions over time.

CHAPTER 5

Business Ownership, Key to Getting What You Want

Japanese Business Culture

The Japanese are very relationship-oriented in business. They rarely consider a 'quick deal' and prefer to cultivate partnerships that will endure. As part of this long-term approach in business relationships, they tend to want to know a great deal about their partners in order to build the trust and loyalty needed to support future business. You may consider many of the details and questions asked to be irrelevant or unrelated to the point at hand, but try to be patient and provide answers for the sake of the business relationship. Religious faith is not often addressed in this culture.

Chinese Business Culture

Negotiation Style: Relationship-Oriented

The Chinese term for negotiation, tan pan, combines two characters that mean 'to discuss' and 'to judge.' From a Chinese point of view, negotiations are mechanisms for building trust and harmony so that both parties can work towards reciprocal benefit. In Chinese business culture, negotiation depends on creating long-term relationships. For example, final negotiations and deals are frequently reached outside of formal meetings, often at restaurants and bars. Religious faith is not often addressed in this culture.

Filipino Business Culture

Personal relationships play a large role in Filipino business culture. Finding a third-party introduction is helpful, as Filipinos prefer to work with those they know and trust. For this reason, nepotism is common. It is also preferred that face-to-face meetings are held when possible, as over-the-phone business is considered impersonal. Religious faith is not often addressed in this culture.

American Indian Business Culture

Navigating business culture in India requires an appreciation of its diverse identities, languages, and customs, intertwined with financial considerations. Greetings often include handshakes or the traditional namaste, reflecting respect and cultural sensitivity. Attire leans towards smart, comfortable clothing, suitable for India's diverse climates. English serves as a lingua franca, yet nuances like indirect refusals ("we'll see") require careful interpretation. The hierarchical structure in Indian businesses emphasizes addressing individuals by their titles and respecting seniority in decision-making, which can influence financial negotiations and budget approvals. Building relationships through small talk and demonstrating patience are crucial, given the importance of trust and intuition alongside financial data. Acknowledging India's regional diversity is essential, as business practices and financial strategies can vary significantly between regions like North and South India. Overall, success in Indian business culture hinges on adapting to local customs, fostering meaningful connections, and navigating financial negotiations with cultural sensitivity.

Hispanic/Mexican Business Culture

In Hispanic/Mexican business culture, personal relationships and family ties are paramount. Building trust and rapport is essential before any business can be conducted. Networking and social interactions, such as shared meals and informal gatherings, are common ways to establish and strengthen business relationships. Mexicans typically prefer face-to-face meetings over virtual communication, as they value personal interaction. Additionally, it is important to show respect for hierarchy and seniority, often addressing people by their titles and surnames.

Negotiations can be lengthy and involve a lot of discussion, as decision-making is usually consensual and may require consultation with various stakeholders. Mexicans often prefer a flexible approach to contracts and agreements, viewing them as adaptable to changing circumstances rather than rigid and final. Punctuality is valued but can be more relaxed compared to American standards. Overall, patience, respect for personal relationships, and a willingness to engage in social interactions are key to successful business dealings in Mexican culture.

CHAPTER 6

Domestic Violence, Emotional Abuse, and Its Affect on the Family

I have been a licensed marriage family therapist in San Diego, CA, for 30 years and have counseled clients of all nationalities. I have found that domestic violence and sexual abuse happen in all cultures. It is a secret that no one talks about. It is the yelling, screaming, and sometimes physical assault by the fathers, and in some cases, it is the mother who follows a learned parental behavior and is the perpetrator. The child is controlled by guilt and a withdrawal of love if they do not accept the violence inflicted upon them. Also, sexual abuse occurs in all cultures when unattended boys start exploring the sexual parts of their sisters, and the child is told to keep quiet to protect the perpetrator. In most cases, it is the male, and in a few cases, I have found a girl who was sexually violated and inflicted forced sexual contact on a female sibling because she experienced a sexual event that was pleasurable and wanted to experience the stimulating pleasure event again.

I have found fathers, grandfathers, uncles, and male cousins have their first sexual experience with a female family member who is afraid she will be blamed for causing the male to have sex with her even though the male is stronger, larger, taller, and usually forces himself or will coerce or manipulate the female to feel she is doing him a favor or, in many cases, has told the girl that if she tells him, he will say she wanted to have the sexual encounter. In all my years of counseling children, women, and men, I have yet to find a young girl with a strong desire to have sex at an early age, unless she was introduced to sex unwillingly by a male perpetrator.

I have had girl children as young as 9 months be sexually abused by their father when their mother went to work and left them alone with their dad. These clients have reported this to me when they came to me as an older child, ages 5 to 18. Although I counseled children as young as 2 years old when I was a therapist working with child protective services clients for 15 years, This is when I often had to rely on my intuitive skills to interpret what the child was saying to me.I used dolls to have them show me what happened to them because they knew something happened of a sexual nature, but they did not have the vocabulary to explain what happened. It broke my heart to see so many girls violated just because they had a vagina, and they did not understand what happened to them. Also, I had boys who were sexually violated as children who were embarrassed to tell anyone what happened to them as children and shared about their sexual trauma as grown men when they came to me in counseling.

Domestic violence in the home is associated with increased isolation from the outside world and limited personal freedom and accessibility to resources. Whenever a woman is placed in physical danger or controlled by the threat or use

Forms of Abuse

Domestic violence is an ongoing, debilitating experience involving physical, psychological, and/or sexual abuse through physical force. The risk of abuse is highest when a woman is separated from supportive networks.

Physical abuse typically recurs and intensifies in both frequency and severity. It may include:

- Pushing, shoving, slapping, punching, kicking, choking
- Assault with a weapon
- Holding, tying down, or restraining her
- Leaving her in dangerous situations
- Refusing to assist when she is sick or injured

Emotional or psychological abuse may precede or accompany physical violence as a means of control through fear and degradation. It may include:

- Threats of harm
- Physical and social isolation

- Extreme jealousy and possessiveness
- Deprivation
- Intimidation
- Degradation and humiliation
- Calling her names and belittling her
- False accusations, blaming her for everything
- Ignoring, dismissing, or ridiculing her needs
- Lying, breaking promises, destroying trust
- Driving fast and recklessly to frighten and intimidate her

Sexual abuse in violent relationships is often the most difficult aspect of abuse for women to discuss. It may include any form of forced sex or sexual degradation, such as:

- Trying to make her perform sexual acts against her will
- Pursuing sexual activity when she is not fully conscious or is unable to consent, or is afraid to say no
- Physically hurting her during sex or assaulting her genitals, including the use of objects or weapons intravaginally, orally, or anally
- Forcing her to have sex without protection against pregnancy or sexually transmitted diseases
- Criticizing her and calling her sexually degrading names

Most of this information can be found in one of my 24 books published by PSI Publishers: Anger Management Skills For Men, Anger Management Skills For Women, Anger Management Skills For Teens, Anger Management Skills For Middle Schools, and Anger Management Skills For Elementary Schools. These books are available on my website at journeytoselflove.com and through Ingram. I offer Counseling and Intuitive Coaching services at 619-262-9951. Visit https://calendly.com/idagreenephd/30min for more information.

CHAPTER 7

Explore Your Unique Intuition Genius

In our journey through understanding and uplifting the ethnic American spirit, we have explored the various facets of our cultural heritage, self-esteem, family dynamics, and financial independence. Each chapter has illuminated the unique challenges and triumphs that shape our identities and strengthen our communities. We have delved into the richness of our cultural traditions, the importance of nurturing our self-worth, the complexities of family relationships, and the strategies for achieving financial stability and growth.

As we reflect on these insights, it becomes clear that the journey towards empowerment and fulfillment is multifaceted. It requires not only an understanding of our external circumstances but also a deep connection with our inner selves. Now, let's take a step further and delve into the power of intuition as a tool for personal and collective transformation. Intuition is an innate gift that resides within each of us, a guiding force that can lead us towards clarity, healing, and empowerment. By harnessing this inner wisdom, we can overcome the obstacles that hold us back and unlock our full potential.

In this chapter, we will explore how to activate and strengthen our intuition, allowing it to guide us in our daily lives. We will learn how to tap into this powerful resource to make informed decisions, manifest our desires, and create a life filled with abundance and joy. Through practical exercises, real-life testimonials, and expert guidance, we will uncover the steps to align with our higher selves and embrace the divine wisdom that flows through us.

Ready to get results like these?

"After shutting off my intuition years ago, I felt as if I had lost my gifts forever. But, within the first week I had regained most of what I had lost. My work with Dr. Ida allows me to work on a much deeper level with my clients and even guides me in finding new clients. I am learning to trust my Intuition as a tool in all areas of my business. I am truly grateful for her insight and guidance!"

~ Becky Hess

"I had lost my intuitive abilities and was able to reestablish my intuition in Dr. Ida's program."

~ Jeanette A. Sotomayor

"Dr. Ida provided valuable information about my business and my life!"

~ Jill Lublin, Publicist, 3X Best Selling Author

Free Yourself From Uncertainty, Worry, And Disempowering Beliefs Holding Back Your Health, Relationships, Or Money

Intuition is a powerful force within each of us, a guiding light that can lead us to clarity, healing, and empowerment. Yet, many of us are disconnected from this inner wisdom, hindered by uncertainty, worry, and limiting beliefs. The Unique Intuition Genius Activation Program is designed to help you reconnect with your intuition and use it to transform every aspect of your life.

Get Clarity & Divine-Guidance

To navigate life's challenges and opportunities, clarity is essential. This program will help you know which path or idea will lead to your desired results and be the most abundant for you. By tapping into your intuition, you will access profound insights that align with your highest good.

Turn On Your "Miracle Magnet"

Manifesting without struggle is possible when you align with the universe's flow. This part of the program teaches you how to open yourself to the Creator's manifestation through you, allowing you to attract positive outcomes effortlessly. You will learn techniques to become a magnet for miracles and positive changes.

Harness Your Personal Power To Heal

Healing is a multifaceted process that involves the body, mind, relationships, and financial well-being. Through this program, you will learn to heal your body, nurture healthier relationships, and overcome financial challenges. The exercises and meditations provided will help you address and heal your deepest wounds.

Here's What You Get

Module 1 - Program Overview To Activate Your Intuition: Go Into The Silence: Understand how your logical mind is holding you back. Tap into your intuition to access the bounty of all that's available to you.

Module 2 - Intuition Activation: Focus on your Intuition through guided exercises and practices.

Module 3 - Read The Energy Of Others: Learn to understand and interpret the energy of those around you.

Intuition Income Activator Assessment

In addition to everything inside the Intuition Activation: Spiritual Initiation Program, I'm also offering a **<u>BONUS</u>** Intuition Assessment session with me. This session is designed to tune up and jump-start your path to allowing, opening, and receiving more. You will experience the flow of more good in your life, bypass your own blocks, and immediately receive all that you need.

To Join

Let's connect one-on-one to discuss how the Unique Intuition Genius Activation can support you in getting clarity, turning on your "Miracle Magnet," and harnessing your power to heal!

Book here: https://calendly.com/idagreenephd/30min. And I'll answer your questions and give you all the information you need to join the Unique Intuition Genius Activation Program. I can't wait for you to experience the life changes waiting for you!

CHAPTER 8

Who Are You, Did We Acknowledge You?

We know you are an essential part of humanity, so let us know if you want your ethnicity or cultural ethnicity included in our next book. We love, value, and appreciate you for being alive and contributing to the world in your own special way. We are glad you were born, and we celebrate you. Please send it to my email: **idagreene@cox.net or idagreene@yahoo.com**

Additional ways we can support you:

- All Channeled Messages From Source/Universe/God/Creator through Dr. Ida
- Soul Life Purpose Reading - for $150, Make payment to Paypal.me/dridagreenee/197
- Secret to Your Life Reading -$197 Make payment to Paypal.me/dridagreenee/197
- Awaken Intuition Activation 1 hour Session $597 Make payment to PayPal.me/dridagreene/597
- https://bit.ly/BOOKDrIda. US Landline phone number 619-262-9951 Cell-Text WhatsApp 619-452-9663

Testimonials Partial List Included

INTUITIVE BUSINESS DIAGNOSTIC SESSION 2015

"I had an Intuitive Business Diagnostic session with Ida Greene, Sales Psychic; I was having feelings of depression that were affected by the business. After my session with her, I felt more energized and alive. I highly recommend her Intuitive Business Diagnostic session."

Rich German, JVIC Founder, Consultant

Here's what **Gina Hussar** said about her FREE Intuitive Business Diagnostic session:

"Today I had an INCREDIBLE session with Ida Greene!! If you are in need of insight on any business or personal situation and have a chance to have a session with her yourself, I highly recommend it!! Her intuitive gifts blow me away. I'm still speechless by the physical changes I felt, and something she mentioned has already happened just four hours later!!! Thank you, Ida! You are a bright light, and I'm blessed to know you!"

11/19/17 TESTIMONIALS

"I recently attended Dr. Ida Greene Intuition, Magic Group Coaching program for Entrepreneurs-Use Your Intuition to Get More Clients, Sales, & Cash Flow. I found the information taught in the program very helpful in my business, and I recommend this program to anyone who wants to incorporate

intuition into their business and life. Thanks, Dr. Ida!"

Jean Fischer, CEO/Visionary

I recently attended Dr. Ida Greene Intuition's Magic Group Coaching program for Entrepreneurs: Use Your Intuition to Get More Clients Sales and Cash Flow. I found the information taught in the program very helpful in my business and I recommend this program to anyone who wants to use their Intuition as a business tool or (incorporate the use of intuition into their business)

Dr. Venus Ramos

"I recently committed time and completed two back-to-back classes over 15 weeks with Dr. Greene.

This was extremely helpful and critical to the development of my intuition in both my personal and business life.

I am in transition in both areas of my life, and God brought me Dr. Greene to help me in my development. I would encourage everybody to utilize this class resource she offers to further your psychological, intuitive and spiritual development."

Scott L. November 2017

"Use Your Intuition to Get More Clients Sales, Cash Flow. I found the information taught in the program very helpful in my business to help me get new clients"

Yvette Bowlin

"I recently attended Dr. Ida Greene Intuition, Magic Group Coaching program for Entrepreneurs-Use Your Intuition to Get More Clients Sales, Cash Flow. Even though I did not have my own business, I found the information taught in the program very helpful in my work life and it helped me in my communications with my supervisor. I feel the techniques taught on how to read the energy field of others is very useful in the workplace or in a personal relationship. I highly recommend this program and the use of intuition as a valuable asset"

Arnetha Booth

ENERGETIC ALIGNMENT TESTIMONIAL

"I recently attended Dr. Ida Greene's Intuition, Magic Group Coaching program for Entrepreneurs-Use Your Intuition to Get More Clients Sales, Cash Flow. I found the Use of the Energetic Alignment helpful in showing me how to keep my body in alignment to be a more powerful leader with my clients and in my business."

Jean Fischer, CEO/Visionary
Peace With Money, LLC

INTUITIVE BUSINESS DIAGNOSTIC SESSION

"I had an Intuitive Business Diagnostic session with Dr. Ida Intuitive Life Coach, the information she shared was helpful for my business and my life."

Dr. Venus Ramos

INTUITION ACTIVATION

"I experienced the Activation of my Intuition in the Intuition, Magic Group Coaching program for Entrepreneurs Your Intuition to Get More Clients Sales, Cash Flow. I felt and enjoyed the Activation of my intuition in the group Coaching program, and I recommend this process to anyone who wants to use their Intuition as a business tool or (incorporate the use of intuition into their business.)"

Yvette Bowlin

"I experienced the Reset The Body's Natural Rhythms in Dr. Ida 's Intuition Magic Group Coaching program for Entrepreneurs. I enjoyed the process and found it very helpful to reset my body's natural rhythm to relieve stress and toxic energy from my body and allow my body to get back into its natural flow. I recommend this process to anyone

who wants to get their body back into its natural energetic flow of peace and harmony."

"1. Energetic Alignment Testimonial

I recently attended Dr. Ida Greene's Intuition, Magic Group Coaching program for Entrepreneurs- Use Your Intuition to Get More Clients Sales, Cash Flow. I found the Use of Energetic Alignment helpful in showing me how to keep my body in alignment to be a more powerful leader with my clients and in my business.

2. Intuitive Business Diagnostic Session I had an Intuitive Business Diagnostic session with Dr. Ida, an Intuitive Life Coach, and the information she shared was helpful for my business and my life.

3. Intuition Activation

I experienced the activation of my intuition in the Intuition Magic Group Coaching program for Entrepreneurs. Use your intuition to get more clients' sales and cash flow. I felt and enjoyed the Activation of my intuition in the group coaching program, and I recommend this process to anyone who wants to use their Intuition as a business tool or (incorporate the use of intuition into their business)

4. Reset Your Body's Natural Rhythms

I experienced the Reset The Body's Natural Rhythms in Dr. Ida 's Intuition Magic Group Coaching program for Entrepreneurs. I enjoyed the process and found it very helpful to reset my body's natural rhythm to relieve stress and toxic energy from my body and allow my body to get back into its natural flow. I recommend this process to anyone who wants to get their body back into its natural, energetic flow of peace and harmony."

Arnetha Booth

Information and Resources

Anger Management Skills for Men. Copyright © August 5, 2003, Second Edition, August 1, 2008, P. S. I. Publishers, 2910 Baily Ave. San Diego, CA 92105. All rights reserved. No part of this publication may be reproduced, distributed, transmitted, transcribed, stored in a retrieval system, or translated into any language without the publisher's express prior agreement and written permission. Other books by the author include Self-Esteem: The Essence of You, Success Now, Soft Power Negotiation Skills™, How to Be a Success In Business, and Light The Fire Within You.

ISBN 1-881165-10-8

Other Resources:

If the patient feels it is safe to do so, provide her with written information (including phone numbers) on legal options, as well as local counseling and crisis intervention services, shelters, and community resources. Additionally, educational materials on domestic violence in waiting areas and examination rooms may help patients identify violence as a personal health problem.

National organizations on domestic violence and many local and state battered women's programs have information available for use in physician offices. The National Domestic Violence Hotline (800 333-SAFE) is a 24-hour resource to help women find local shelters. Counselors speak Spanish as well as English. The National Woman Abuse Prevention Center (202-857-0216) publishes fact sheets on domestic violence, a quarterly newsletter, and a series of brochures. Some of the material is translated into Spanish and Polish. The American College of Obstetricians and Gynecologists (202-863-2518) publishes "The Abused Woman," a publication for patients. The Family Violence Prevention Fund (415-821-4553) provides direct services to victims and develops public policy and training programs.

Local domestic violence shelters and statewide domestic violence programs are frequently listed in the phone book. They can help with housing information.

Final Thoughts

Please consider the role you can play to uplift the Ethnic American Spirit so we can become a living embodiment of people who uplift the Ethnic American Spirit for all Americans regardless of race, creed, or color. It is time for us to realize that we are all member of the human race, brothers and sister. It is time for us to become more tolerant of the religious and cultural practices of each other and genuinely love each other.

INDEX

BIBLIOGRAPHY

Anzaldua, G. (1987). Borderlands/La Frontera: The New Mestiza. San Francisco: Aunt Lute Books.

Baldwin, J. (1963). The Fire Next Time. New York: Dial Press.

Coates, T. (2015). Between the World and Me. New York: Spiegel & Grau.

Collins, P. H. (2000). Black Feminist Thought: Knowledge, Consciousness, and the Politics of Empowerment. New York: Routledge.

Cultural Atlas. (n.d.). Chinese Culture: Business Culture. Retrieved from https://culturalatlas.sbs.com.au/chinese-culture/chinese-culture-business-culture#chinese-culture-business-culture

Cultural Atlas. (n.d.). Filipino Culture: Business Culture. Retrieved from https://culturalatlas.sbs.com.au/filipino-culture/filipino-culture-business-culture#filipino-culture-business-culture

Cultural Atlas. (n.d.). Japanese Culture: Family. Retrieved from https://culturalatlas.sbs.com.au/japanese-culture/japanese-culture-family

Davis, A. Y. (1981). Women, Race, & Class. Random House.

Du Bois, W. E. B. (1903). The Souls of Black Folk. Chicago: A.C. McClurg & Co.

Fanon, F. (1961). The Wretched of the Earth. New York: Grove Press.

Freire, P. (1970). Pedagogy of the Oppressed. New York: Continuum.

Greene, Dr. Ida. "Uplifting The Ethnic American Spirit." P. S. I. Publishers, 2024.

HispanicAd. (n.d.). How Culture Affects Perception of Money. Retrieved from https://hispanicad.com/news/how-culture-affects-perception-money/

King, M. L. Jr. (1963). Strength to Love. New York: Harper & Row. hooks, b. (2000). All About Love: New Visions. New York: William Morrow & Co.

Morrison, T. (1987). Beloved. New York: Alfred A. Knopf.

National Association for the Advancement of Colored People (NAACP). (n.d.).
History. Retrieved from
https://www.naacp.org/history/

Said, E. W. (1978). Orientalism. New York: Pantheon Books.

Takaki, R. (1989). Strangers from a Different Shore: A History of Asian Americans. New York: Little, Brown and Company.

Tatum, B. D. (1997). Why Are All the Black Kids Sitting Together in the Cafeteria? And Other Conversations About Race. New York: Basic Books.

United States Census Bureau. (n.d.). Demographic Trends in the 20th Century. Retrieved from https://www.census.gov/history/

Wikipedia contributors. (n.d.). Culture of Asia. In Wikipedia, The Free Encyclopedia. Retrieved from
https://en.wikipedia.org/wiki/Culture_of_Asia

Wikipedia contributors. (n.d.). History of Asia. In Wikipedia, The Free Encyclopedia. Retrieved from
https://en.wikipedia.org/wiki/History_of_Asia

Zinn, H. (1980). A People's History of the United States. New York: Harper & Row.

www.ingramcontent.com/pod-product-compliance
Lightning Source LLC
Chambersburg PA
CBHW041929040426
42445CB00018B/1948